The Greatest Leader
He Ever Saw

The Greatest Leader He Ever Saw

A STORY OF CHARACTER-BASED LEADERSHIP

Michael F Andrew

Author of *How to Think like a CEO and Act like a Leader*

ISBN: 1517660718
ISBN 13: 9781517660710
Library of Congress Control Number: 2015916545
CreateSpace Independent Publishing Platform
North Charleston, South Carolina

Character is destiny.
—Heraclitus, Greek philosopher, 535–475 BCE

Character is the foundation of all worthwhile success.
—John Hays Hammond, early twentieth-century industrialist

True leadership starts with the heart – with character.
— John C. Maxwell, *Today Matters*

To Michael Todd Andrew, my life blessing, who allowed me to experience a father's love and the strength of a child's spirit.

Author's Note

have spent many years all over the world and in the United States as an executive, a business owner, and a consultant to senior executives. The result of all this is my own personal journey, where my learning is still far from over. We all continue to have so much to learn. I have studied and observed leaders for a number of years now. I guess you could say it is my "practice," just as doctors become more expert in their medical practices and specialty areas.

So, in my years as a corporate executive and working with, managing, developing, and coaching staff members and leaders, I have come to realize that leadership starts with certain fundamentals. Those fundamentals are based on character. I don't care if a leader has a great vision, or if a leader excels in a variety of "competencies" that the HR world seems to be consumed with.

As a well-known thought leader, Peter Senge, once said, "It is not what the vision is; it is what the vision does." I am more concerned that a leader can make things happen while doing so with integrity.

Integrity. This is where character comes in.

If you Google the word *leadership*, you will come up with millions of links. Also, if you go on a social site like LinkedIn and pose the question, "How would you define leadership?" you will see that everyone has an opinion on leadership and what a good leader looks like. That is what makes the field of leadership development so challenging. Everyone has a view, and it's based on each person's experience with good leaders and bad leaders.

If I ask you, the reader, "Who is the best leader or manager you ever worked for?" you will instantly think of someone. If you are lucky, you will think of more than one.

If I then ask, "What made that person such a good manager or leader?" you will also be able to write down a list of qualities or characteristics that made him or her so good.

Of course, we can all answer the reverse question: "Who is the worst leader or manager you ever worked for?" You will be able to answer with specifics why this person was a terrible leader or manager. Most of it comes down to behavior that, to me, is reflective of character.

So, in my humble and simplistic view, leadership is about achieving results consistently and doing so with integrity.

This story is about the integrity part. I call it "character-based leadership," which is about the quality of one's character. I have come to believe that integrity, humility, and treating people with dignity are the foundations of character-based leaders.

I hope you find the lessons practical and not conceptual or theoretical. You will know if they are practical because you will be able to apply these character-based leadership lessons immediately in your work and, more important, in your life. You don't have to be a CEO or senior executive because character-based leadership is about leading from within, from who you are, at whatever stage you are in your career. In fact, these character-based lessons are just as relevant in our personal lives as well.

Michael F. Andrew
Riyadh, Saudi Arabia
Dubai, UAE
Laconia, New Hampshire, USA
mfandrew@aol.com
http://www.leadershipauthor.com

Acknowledgments

I am grateful for how things usually work out for the best. In that spirit, I appreciate those who gave me opportunities and those who did not. To those who gave me the opportunities, I will always be grateful for your confidence and for allowing me to grow personally and professionally. To those who did not give me opportunities, those closed doors opened new and better doors and allowed me to learn important life and career lessons while achieving more than I ever dreamed, including my current dream opportunity with Al Faisaliah Group. I send special regards to my friends and colleagues at Al Faisaliah Group and our operating companies.

To my sister, Karen Andrew, who took the time to review the original manuscript and whose feedback allowed me to change some aspects of the key characters and gave me the idea for the role of Addie.

To Marsha Johnson ("Mrs. J") and her sister Sherry Fox, who enthusiastically went through each and every page with detailed edits and provided very welcomed encouragement.

To Tinus Van de Merwe, my South African colleague who read the real rough draft of the manuscript and gave such heartfelt and valued feedback.

To my colleague Thamer Al Eisa and his wife for researching parts of the Koran for me for key lessons that are relevant to this story.

To my colleague Mohammed Al Hajri for developing some incredible and creative cover ideas and for graciously taking the time to help me think through the decision for the book cover.

About the Story and the Characters

This story is a fable about an arrogant, ignorant, and selfish billionaire who is not at all liked nor respected. He is a terrible leader. At one point during his life, he becomes inspired by someone who works in his organization who is both very well liked *and* respected, achieves results, and is always looked to as a leader. This billionaire businessman decides to discover and learn why this person is such a great leader, the greatest leader he ever saw. What results is a transformation in character, leadership, and humility just as profound as the character transformation of Charles Dickens's infamous character, Ebenezer Scrooge.

So this story is pure fiction, a fable, as are all of the characters. I use this fable to illustrate that leadership can be very powerful when it is based on a foundation of integrity and humility and treating people with dignity. It is about a leader who cares for others and is willing to serve the greater good, one who is selfless and not self-serving. Coach John Wooden was the renowned basketball coach who led UCLA to ten NCAA championships. His success as a coach is historic and legendary. But Wooden is more recognized by all his former players and all who knew him as a man of integrity, a man of character. I love what Mr. Wooden once said; it is also relevant to the story you are about to read: "Be more concerned with your character than your reputation because your character is what you really are, while your reputation is merely what others think you are."

Present Day

Todd Ferragamo, Professional Baseball Player

I t was the seventh and deciding game of the World Series. The series was tied at three games each. It was the bottom of the ninth inning, the final game to determine the World Series championship, and it was down to the final out.

Todd Ferragamo, from the American League team, was at the plate. He was the last person anyone—the fans and, honestly, even his coaches and teammates—wanted at the plate at this time. His team was losing 3–1 with runners on first and second, two outs, and a 0–2 count.

Todd was far from a star. He was an adequate utility player at best, available in reserve when any of the starting infielders were hurt. This had been his role for the last eleven years. A thirty-five-year-old veteran with a nondescript and humble career, he was a .237 lifetime hitter with only five career home runs who was fairly dependable defensively, which is always a minimum and a must for an infielder. He was not a household name. He never would be. He certainly would never be considered for any TV commenting role in the future, just as he was never approached for any local TV commercials or speaking appearances at the local schools and communities. He was amazed and even grateful for having a major league professional baseball career. His jersey was never manufactured for sale, and his baseball card was never in demand. He was outstanding in his high school and college days, but this was major-league professional baseball. It was a stretch to call his career even modest. He played only when others were hurt. He did not hit for power. He did not even hit for singles much, for that matter.

There were many other players more deserving to be in the big leagues than Todd Ferragamo. But his teammates loved him, and they elected him captain for seven years in a row. The workers in the clubhouse loved him, and that meant more to Todd than even the respect from his teammates, most of whom he respected, except for those with out-of-place egos. But it was the owner of the team, Mr. Stuart Holbrook, who admired him even more than anyone else. Mr. Holbrook, who had inherited much of his wealth from his father—quadrupling his fortune with savvy investments in hedge funds, trading in commodities, and being a major shareholder in three successful software firms—saw something in Todd far more important than baseball skills, something he honestly knew he lacked but wished he had. It was only because of this owner that Todd was still in the major leagues.

The team's general manager and coaches had stopped trying to convince Holbrook years ago that the team would be better off with a more productive utility player, one who could hit for better average and power, and with more speed and possibly even better defense. Stuart Holbrook would never consider removing Todd Ferragamo from the team, and he would not budge on that point. The players and coaches would wonder why, though they casually accepted it because Todd was such a good teammate. Stuart Holbrook clearly knew why.

Yet even the owner had to second-guess himself now, in the bottom of the ninth inning, with his team losing the game 3–1 and on the verge of losing the World Series, and with Ferragamo at the plate with a count of 0–2, no balls, and two strikes. He was at the plate because he was called to play shortstop when the starting shortstop, Ramon Ruiz, jammed his ankle sliding into second base on an attempted steal in game six. To make matters worse, the manager had already exhausted the two adequate pinch hitters in the seventh and eighth innings trying to create some momentum while looking for a base hit with runners in scoring position.

Todd stepped away from the batter's box after he looked at two blazing fastballs whiz past him for strikes. In what was the most crucial moment in his baseball career, all Todd could do was take a deep breath, get back in the batter's box, and try to stop his right leg from shaking from nerves. As he prepared for this major event with over one hundred million people watching around the world, he was reminded of the quote by John F. Kennedy in his book *Profiles in Courage*: "Courage is not the absence of fear. It is taking action in the presence of fear." Todd Ferragamo was not just fearful. He was frightened, but he had no choice but to face the fear, try, and hope.

Then it happened. It happened so quickly and unexpectedly. If you had glanced at the scoreboard, looked down to find your drink, or glanced at your mobile phone to see if there were any messages, you would have missed it. Fifty-seven thousand fans in the stadium and millions of people glued to the TV would never forget this moment, a lifetime ESPN highlight moment. Todd Ferragamo's life changed forever in that one split second, as life often does for better or for worse. Just in that one split second.

The opposing pitcher, a perennial all-star generally considered the best closer in the game, earning $21 million per year, towering six foot six inches with an intimidating fastball that could reach ninety-eight miles per hour, used his best pitch, the fastball, but this time put even more behind his windup and released with what he was sure was his last pitch to end the game. That pitch was clocked at an amazing 103 miles per hour. He was ready to raise his two hands in the air, get hugged first by the catcher, and then be mobbed by all of his teammates on the pitcher's mound.

With no balls and two strikes behind him, Todd Ferragamo knew it would be a fastball. He knew it would be pure unmatched power against his very limited major-league skills from such an undistinguished career as a mediocre utility player. The dynamics of the ball hurled at 103 miles per hour allowed it to take less than three seconds to easily clear the left-field wall, about fifteen rows up, after Todd's swing connected with the ball. The left fielder never moved. Actually, the left fielder was too stunned to move.

The final score was 4–3, a walk-off home run with a hero's welcome by not just the players but out-of-control fans greeting him at home plate. It was reminiscent of Bobby Thompson's momentous ninth-inning, two-out, walk-off home run to lead the Brooklyn Dodgers over the New York Giants in 1954. Or Pittsburgh's Bill Mazeroski's walk-off home run in the ninth inning of the 1960 World Series to beat the powerful New York Yankees. It was going to be an ESPN highlight for the ages.

It was a miracle! Todd Ferragamo was the unexpected hero. His team was now the World Series champions, and Stuart Holbrook had won his first World Series after twenty-three years as owner of the team.

Stuart Holbrook was proud of what his player had just done. His love and respect and admiration for Todd Ferragamo had nothing to do with this historic home run. He was pleased beyond his dreams for what had just occurred. Almost every major-league baseball player, past and present, had more successful careers than Todd Ferragamo, but every one of those players would have traded their entire careers to do what Todd Ferragamo had just done to become an iconic part of sports history.

As Todd Ferragamo rounded third base on his way home to immortality, he wasn't thinking about his teammates or the fans, and certainly not the media and the hero's welcome that would come as the city celebrated this momentous event. No. He spoke quietly to his older sister, Adrielle, or "Addie," who'd died years earlier from a rare form of leukemia. It was Addie who influenced and inspired him to transform his sordid life of drugs and alcohol and a track record of irresponsible behavior. She was undoubtedly the personal hero in Todd's life. She was his true north. Todd still mourned his dear sister, whom he missed every day. He realized every day that it was Addie who had changed his life to be the man he was today.

The market value of Stuart Holbrook's team increased precipitously. It was incredible timing because at seventy-seven years old, he was preparing to sell the team and retire. Three months later, the commissioner of Major League Baseball approved the sale of the team for $1.1 billion. Stuart Holbrook had paid $23 million for the team twenty-three years earlier.

Two days later, he readjusted his will.

Eight years later, at eighty-five years old, Stuart Holbrook died peacefully in his sleep.

Years Earlier

Stuart Holbrook, Billionaire and Owner of the Team

Everyone wished they were in Stuart Holbrook's shoes. He was a billionaire who was often showcased in *Forbes*, *Fortune*, the *Wall Street Journal*, and the *Financial Times*. He had everything: countless commercial and residential properties, a private jet, and a 170-foot yacht with a full-time crew of twelve. He had no children, though he was on his fourth marriage.

Stuart Holbrook wished he was like Todd Ferragamo. Since Todd had joined his big-league team, Holbrook had always noticed the way he paid attention to the workers in the clubhouse—those who cleaned the clubhouse, those who cleaned the players' uniforms every day, those who made the travel arrangements, the administrative staff, the security in the ballpark, the vendors who sold the food and drinks, and the crew who maintained the impeccable field. He was a perfect teammate.

Holbrook saw something in Todd that he couldn't put his finger on. He observed how Todd was not just respected but was liked as well. As for himself, he knew that people acted as if they liked him because he was Stuart Holbrook, one of the wealthiest people in the world. Of course, people would appear to like him. But it was not genuine, not like it was with Todd Ferragamo. He knew, deep down, that people did not like him. Nor did they respect him; it was his money they respected, and it was only his money that had any sort of influence. Being wealthy was not the least bit fulfilling for Stuart Holbrook. Yes, he had everything one could want materially, and he was blind to his faults, but he knew that if he did not have wealth, people would be much more obvious in their disrespect for him. Most people who had dealings with him simply despised him and his rude, cold, and arrogant manner.

Holbrook loved being the owner of a professional baseball team. He just wished he had those qualities that made Todd Ferragamo a...that was it! A leader. Todd Ferragamo was not a famous name in the sports world. He was simply a journeyman baseball player who made very little income, relatively speaking, for a professional athlete. He was not a star; he was not a hero. His role consisted mainly of staying in shape, practicing before each game, and then sitting on the bench for about 80 percent of the games, playing only when one of the starting infielders was hurt or needed a rest. But he was a leader. He was loved and respected.

So Stuart Holbrook decided to start a journey to find out what it was that made Todd Ferragamo the greatest leader he ever saw. He bought a journal and started writing down the stories as he made efforts to learn.

Adrielle "Addie" Ferragamo, Todd's Sister

Todd grew up adoring his older sister, Addie. His love for her was unwavering. She was his idol. It was as if she did and said everything right. She was the sweetest sister, but she knew when to be tough. "Don't ever mistake my kindness for weakness," she would say to her brother when it was needed. A very good athlete herself, Addie was the one who taught Todd how to play baseball, a sport he fell in love with, when he was a young boy. Yet, in spite of Addie's influence, Todd, with his awesome athletic prowess as a high school and college athlete, became entangled in hubris and the uncontrolled abuse of alcohol and drugs while having fun bullying kids who weren't cool.

While Addie was away at medical school, she wasn't around to see Todd's day-to-day behavior, though she knew something was wrong when he wouldn't return her calls. Their parents were too naïve to notice anything. When Addie was home during one of her semester breaks, she observed firsthand the damage he was doing to his health and well-being. In fact, there was no well-being.

"Toddy, I love you as much as a sister can love a brother. I see the greatest potential in you! Imagine combining your potential and talent with hard work, discipline, and a goal? You have the whole world in the palm of your hand! Most people on this planet would love to have what you have and be who you are. You are a very good young man, Todd, and you are losing who you are and what you can be." Addie was firm but far from finished. She walked right up to his face and with a force he never realized existed in her, she said, "You are going to turn your life around NOW! Do you hear me, Brother?!"

Todd was hiding his fear and embarrassment when he replied, "What do you know? I am better than any athlete in the state even if I'm blindfolded. I know what I am doing!"

"You don't have any clue, Todd! I am demanding—for the first time in my life—that you stop, or aside from the consequences from me, you will suffer the consequences of a sad life of someone who had it all and wasted it. And remember one thing: how you treat people from all walks of life ultimately says everything about you."

Todd did not change that day. He continued bullying for no good reason. He would make fun of other boys who were poor athletes, shove them against the lockers in the hallway, and embarrass them publicly with his ridicule. Basically, Todd had no interpersonal sensitivity whatsoever for the damage he caused many a young man from his bullying. Then, there were the drinking and the drugs that made him an arrogant and vicious person to be around although he did not realize it. Profound change, transformation, would not begin to be realized until months later when Addie started getting sick. Very sick. It turned out to be a rare form of leukemia. What did change that day Addie yelled at him was a little flame in his heart. The one person who loved him unconditionally, more than anyone aside from his mother and father, was Addie. In his eyes, no one was smarter, more decent, and more genuine than his sister, to whom he looked up with such deep affection, love, and admiration. But as a boy, he'd never had the sense to tell her so.

Todd Ferragamo developed himself into a most highly regarded athlete in his home state while transforming himself into a young man with character. It was character he learned from looking up to the light of his life, his dear sister, Addie, who had the inimitable qualities of strength and leadership and love.

Todd's transformation into not just a greater athlete but also a young man with character coincided with the time when Addie was fighting for her life. She was dying without losing her endless human spirit and her love and hope for her younger brother.

Neither of them had any idea how her legacy would live on in a boundless and profound way.

Norm Sullivan, Clubhouse Manager

"Hi, Mr. Holbrook," said a concerned Norm Sullivan as he was invited into Holbrook's office at the baseball stadium. They had a game later that night. "You wanted to see me?" He never stepped foot on this floor, never mind being invited into the office of the owner. Like everyone else, he didn't like Stuart Holbrook. For the last fifteen years, Norm, or as they called him in Boston, "Nawm," had been the clubhouse manager, responsible for ensuring that the clubhouse, where the players dressed and showered, was always clean, with plenty of soap and clean towels, clean showers, and clean toilets, and that the pregame and postgame food was delivered on time by the outside catering company. He had seen Mr. Holbrook before some games and after some big wins. In all that time, Mr. Holbrook never looked his way or even said hello. Norm remembered the time when he bumped into the owner as he was carrying a pile of clean towels into the clubhouse. Norm had no choice but to respectfully and politely say, "Hello, Mr. Holbrook." All he remembered was the owner not making eye contact with him or even acknowledging him. "What a jerk," Norm said to himself, using a term shared by anyone else who met their owner.

Norm Sullivan was proud of his job. His wife, his three children, and his friends, relatives, and neighbors were proud of Norm and loved talking to him about the inside stories of the players and coaches. But never once did Stuart Holbrook acknowledge his existence.

"Tell me what you know about Todd Ferragamo."

Norm was confused. He felt like this was some sort of investigation. "Excuse me, sir?"

"Tell me about Todd Ferragamo!" Holbrook's tone was forceful and consistent with his everyday behavior, which he could always get away with simply because he was the owner, the billionaire. He had a position of power. "I'm not interested in your views of him as an athlete, but as a person."

Norm was nervous and hesitant as he spoke for the first time to Stuart Holbrook. Norm quickly thought of a story that personified the team captain. He told Stuart about an interaction he'd had with Todd a couple of weeks earlier—a story that still put tears in his eyes when he told it.

❖ ❖ ❖

"Hey, Nawm! How are *you* today?" asked Todd Ferragamo. It was Todd's typical greeting with his strong Boston accent; he had grown up just outside the city.

"Hey, Toddy, ready for the game today?" asked Norm with a smile that conveyed affection.

"I am, Nawm. But the best part of the game is spending time with you guys," said Todd. "If it wasn't for men like you, Nawm, I don't know how any of us would get through these long seasons."

"We feel the same way about players like you, Toddy." Many people called him that.

"Our job is easy, Nawm. We get to do what we love. Believe me, you don't know how much I appreciate everything you do for us. You are the best at what you do!"

"Thanks, Toddy."

"By the way, Nawm, how is your youngest son? You told me he was trying out for the high school basketball team."

Norm hesitated, a little saddened. "Teddy got cut. He's very disappointed. I keep telling him that there's always next year."

Todd listened, nodded, and asked a few questions about why he got cut. Norm told him he was big but too slow and not as skilled as the others, but he played his heart out. He loved the game and loved playing with his friends on the team. Todd listened and came up with an idea that he would not share with Norm at that time.

Todd was a professional baseball player. Although he would not have been able to articulate the concept of maintaining a person's dignity or positively affecting his or her self-esteem, that's what he did naturally.

Norm just loved the guy. When people asked Norm about the personalities of the different players, he always said it was Todd Ferragamo who stood above them all when it came to decency. "You can't find a nicer, more humble person than Ferragamo," Norm would always tell his family, friends, and acquaintances. "They picked the right guy to be captain of the team."

The next day, a Saturday, Norm got a call on his mobile phone. "Hi, Nawm; it's Todd Ferragamo."

Why is he calling me on a Saturday morning when I'll see him tonight at the ballpark? Norm was asking himself.

"Listen, Nawm, is Teddy there? Do you mind if I talk to him for a minute?"

Teddy was amazed that Todd Ferragamo, the captain of his hometown baseball team, called his father on his mobile phone at home. A stammered hi was all fifteen-year-old Teddy Sullivan could muster.

"Hey, Teddy; it's Todd Ferragamo. How are you, pal?"

Teddy still could not believe that he was getting this call. "OK, I guess, Mr. Ferragamo."

"Please call me Todd, OK? Teddy, I heard you got cut from the basketball team. I'm sorry to hear that."

Teddy was very embarrassed. It killed him to get cut, but it was even worse that many people in school were going to know.

"Do you know that Michael Jordan got cut from his high school basketball team?" asked Todd.

"He did?"

"Yes. What happened to Michael Jordan's basketball career?"

Teddy did not even have to answer that question.

"Do you know that I never made a little-league team until I was eleven? And that I got cut from the Babe Ruth team my first year, and that I also got cut from my college team one year?"

"Really?" Teddy was shocked.

"I hear you love the game of basketball. Is that true?"

"Yes, sir. I mean, yes, Todd. I love it. But I'm not good enough, I guess."

"Do you think you're good enough?" Todd asked.

"Kinda; I don't know; I guess so," responded Teddy, a little embarrassed and nervous.

"Do you want to know what I think, Teddy?"

"OK."

"From talking to your dad—he played high school basketball, correct?"

Though he was on the phone, Teddy just nodded yes.

"So he knows the game. He tells me that you don't hesitate to get into the action, that you don't shy away from wanting the ball and going for the rebound. Is that true?"

"I guess so," Teddy still did not know what to say.

"Well, if you love the game, and if you play with your heart like I heard you do, then keep at it—just like Michael Jordan, just like me when I got cut, just like Babe Ruth when he not only broke the record for most home runs but also broke the record for most strikeouts. Keep enjoying the game, have fun, and play with your friends. Keep practicing. I hope to hear another success story from you, Teddy."

"Thank you, Mr. Ferragamo—I mean Todd," said Teddy with tears of inspiration and joy.

"One more thing, Teddy. And this is far more important than basketball."

Teddy waited.

"You are a great kid. The few times I've seen you at the games, I can see how polite you are and that you have a great life ahead of you, far beyond basketball. I respect and admire that about you very much. And I know how much you are loved by your parents. You have many blessings."

Now Teddy could not hold back the tears. He could barely register a thank-you without all-out crying.

"Take care, Teddy, and I hope to see you in the clubhouse soon."

Every player on the varsity basketball team wished they had a relationship with Todd Ferragamo like Teddy Sullivan did.

It was a day Teddy Sullivan never forgot. It was also a day his father, Norm, never forgot.

"I don't know what religion Todd practices, or if he is religious at all," said Norm, "but I remember reading a quote from the Dalai Lama that I know Todd lives his life by, even if he's never heard it. The quote is, 'My religion is simple. My religion is kindness.' That is what I love about Ferragamo."

It was one of many stories that Stuart Holbrook had heard. But now as he started his journey to learn, he added this story to his journal.

Lino Fernandez, Travel Secretary; Madison Robinson, Travel Office Staff; and Reginald Robinson, Madison's Father

"Hello; this is Lino," said Lino Fernandez, the team travel secretary, as he answered his office phone. He saw the call was coming from Stuart Holbrook's office. He assumed that Mr. Holbrook's secretary must be checking up on the flight arrangements for next week's trip to Cleveland and Chicago.

"Lano, this is Stuart Holbrook. Come up to my office. I'd like to speak with you," said the owner in his unfeeling tone and, of course, mispronouncing his name.

Lino hung up the phone. He had no idea what was going on. He never got a call from Stuart Holbrook. Holbrook's secretary would normally have called, not the owner personally. He assumed the worst. He went through all the travel arrangements for the upcoming road trip in his mind, as well as the cost of the trip and his year-to-date actual costs against his budget. He could not think of any glaring problem that would warrant the team owner's requesting his presence in his office. In fact, he never came close to the owner's office. Lino took the stairs to the third floor. His stomach hadn't been this nervous since his Catholic-school days when he was called to the office of the principal, a very stern and intimidating Catholic nun, for punishment.

What the heck is this about? he wondered. He couldn't think of any mistake he had made or anything bad that he'd done, but he assumed the worst. "And he calls me 'Lano.' He doesn't even know my name."

"Lano, come in and sit down," ordered the owner.

Lino was too nervous to correct the big boss about his mispronunciation of his name and let it go at that. His job was too important for him and his family.

Holbrook got right to the point. There were no pleasantries about Lino's family or his job. Actually, he had no idea—nor did he care—whether Lino had a family or not. "What can you tell me about Todd Ferragamo?"

Lino was puzzled. This had nothing to do with his job. *What is this about? Why is he asking me about one of the players?* he asked himself. "What do you mean, sir? He's a good team player, and he's a good captain, if that's what you mean."

"I know that. I want to know what is he like as a person—as a leader or captain."

"Is he in trouble or something, Mr. Holbrook?" Lino was puzzled.

"No" was the rather abrupt reply. "Would you say he is a leader?"

"A leader? I know a little bit about leadership, Mr. Holbrook, from my military days, and if I had to pick a person who is a genuine leader, it would be Todd Ferragamo, sir." Lino Fernandez was a retired major from the Philippine Army and was now a proud US citizen.

"Why do you say that? What has he done for you to say that?" Holbrook was sincerely curious. He wanted to learn.

"Well, for one, sir, he is respected and liked—no wait, I would say loved—by everyone…not just his teammates, but every single member of my staff. He gives everyone the time of day; he knows the names of every person on my staff. The entire travel department loves the guy. He has helped everyone with a kind or encouraging word, with compliments on the work we do. He seems to realize how complicated our work is to make travel arrangements for the entire team and coaching staff, to be 100 percent accurate with the flight and hotel arrangements, with all the equipment accounted for. The phrase 'thank you' is probably the most commonly used one in his vocabulary."

Holbrook was writing fast in his journal. "Go on, Lano."

Lino hesitated, not sure if he should tell the next story. But he felt he had to. "Do you know Madison Robinson?"

Holbrook shook his head. Not a surprise to Lino. "She works for me in the travel office. Her father, Reginald, had a stage-3 non-Hodgkin's lymphoma. Todd paid for his chemotherapy. Thank God, Mr. Robinson is in remission today, thanks to Ferragamo's generosity."

"What? He paid for this man's chemotherapy?"

"Yes. Her father had no insurance coverage with his construction job. Please don't ever tell him I told you. Not even his teammates know. He cares for people far more than he cares for baseball, and I know how much he loves baseball, Mr. Holbrook."

"Hmm, interesting. Tell me more about him," demanded Holbrook as he continued taking notes in his journal.

"He once told me about a quote he heard. I remember this clearly. He said, "'You know, Lino, people who look up to God rarely look down on people.' I never forgot him saying that to me. If anyone lives by that principle, it's Ferragamo."

Lino Fernandez flashed back to that exact moment during the last season as if it happened yesterday. He remembered Todd getting to the ballpark an hour early to meet with Madison at her desk in the travel department. He remembered the concern, the empathy, and the questions as he sought to understand her father's condition and spirits. He remembered Madison crying the whole time she was sharing the story of her father's situation.

Todd spent most of the remaining time learning about her father, Reginald Robinson: his job as a construction worker, the model father he was, and the devoted husband and father he was to Madison and her four siblings. Lino remembered the most genuine care and concern in Todd's face, and the wetness in his eyes. He remembered Todd hugging Madison and telling her how blessed she was to have such a family and such a good father. Madison had cried even harder the next day when she told Lino, her boss, how Todd Ferragamo called her father that night. Her father, suffering from his cancer, was on cloud nine, having gotten the surprising call. She swore it lifted her father's spirits so much that nothing was going to stop him from fighting. The family never knew who the "anonymous" donor was who paid for all of the chemotherapy. Even the doctors and staff kept their word and kept the donor anonymous.

"How do you know he was the one who donated the money?" At this point Holbrook stopped writing and just listened intently.

"I knew," Lino quickly replied. "I just knew. I had no doubt. And I asked Todd. He admitted it to me but asked me never ever to tell anyone."

Stuart Holbrook went back to his note taking. "Any other stories?"

"Yes, sir. I have plenty. I remember he and I were talking and I was telling him about the way he cares for others. He just could not understand the big deal, as if we are all here to care for others. I remember he shared another quote. He said to me, 'Lino, Theodore Roosevelt said, "People don't care how much you know until they know how much you care."' Don't you think that is more important than someone who can hit home runs or can strike out ten in a game?"

Stuart Holbrook kept writing.

"Finally, Mr. Holbrook"—Lino Fernandez was actually enjoying this unexpected meeting; he was amazed that Stuart Holbrook was taking the time to learn about the goodness of his least important player in terms of talent and productivity—"there is a reason he is captain of the team."

Stuart Holbrook stopped taking his notes again to look up and listen to what was coming next.

"It is ironic that Todd Ferragamo is probably the lowest-paid player on the team. Sorry, Mr. Holbrook, I know that's none of my business, but it's part of the story. Everyone knows the highest-paid player is Nick 'Big Dude' McGuire." Lino had a smile on his face and chuckled a little as he began this next story. "Todd is five foot eight inches tall, the smallest guy on the team. Big Dude is six foot four inches and built like a rock with, I might say, the ego to match his size. I've only seen one person confront Big Dude."

"Ferragamo?"

"Yes. Even the coaches treat Big Dude with kid gloves. The other players just can't be bothered getting involved. They seem to ignore or accept Big Dude's ego and self-serving attitude. I don't blame them."

"Huh." The owner remembered how much he paid Nick McGuire—one of the highest, if not the highest, salary in base-ball. All because of his home-run-hitting prowess.

"Well, a few years ago in spring training in Florida, we had an exhibition game with the St. Louis Cardinals. I was sitting on the bench, detailing the team trip the next day to north-ern Florida. All of a sudden I heard Big Dude yelling at some young kid who was about ten or eleven years old. The boy was all excited when he saw Big Dude near the dugout, and he asked him for his autograph. The boy was yelling, 'Big Dude! Big Dude! Over here! Can I have your autograph?' Then Big

Dude starts yelling at the young kid as if he'd hit him over the head with a bat or something. He starts yelling, 'Hey, you! Who do you think you are? My name is Nick. I am too busy to be signing any autographs!'

"Then Big Dude starts yelling at the boy's father for allowing the kid to be so rude. Everyone is watching this, and no one is saying anything or doing anything. It was like everyone was afraid of Big Dude. Except Todd."

Stuart Holbrook had to hear this one. He had to hear how little Todd Ferragamo confronted Big Dude. "So what happened?"

"Todd just casually and in a confident way walked up to Big Dude, started screaming and swearing at him. This went on for a few minutes. Eventually, things calmed down and Todd put his hand on his shoulder, and said something that none of us could hear. When he was done talking to Big Dude, Todd walked back to the infield, and he saw me looking at him. He just winked at me. The next thing I see is Big Dude walking over to the boy and apologizing. He signed the scorecard the boy was carrying, and he also signed a baseball and gave it to the boy. Then he shook the boy's father's hand."

Holbrook was as curious as he'd ever been. "What did he do or say to make Big Dude apologize and sign his autograph?"

"I asked Todd after the game in the locker room. He said, 'Lino, we all know Big Dude's behavior and ego. But I have found that oftentimes bullies don't realize they are being bullies. They have been allowed to get away for so long with their bully behaviors that when someone stands up to them, they seem shocked that they're behaving badly. Big Dude was shocked when I told him the effect his behavior had on that young boy. Why he didn't have a clue to his behavior is something I can't answer. No one wanted to confront him, so I did, for the sake of that young boy. And we all know these fans pay our salaries.'

"Then I asked Todd, 'But what did you say to him? How did you do it? He seemed so gentle with you, Todd,'" Lino went on.

"He said, I did not handle it well at first. My initial approach, using 'f-words,' made things worse and then I realized I was reverting to my old childhood behavior. I was a real jerk about it. So, I adapted to how my sister modeled for me when she came down on me. 'It's not so much what I said, Lino; there was no magic in my words. I approached him by dealing with the issue, his behavior—being specific with what his behavior was and the effect it had on the little boy, and I told him in a respectful manner. I call it *treating issues coldly and people warmly*. They are not mutually exclusive. You confront the issue directly, or in the case of Big Dude, I confronted his behavior, but I did it in a respectful manner. Like most of us, Lino, Big Dude does has a good heart deep inside.

"'His ego hides whatever personal weaknesses or insecurities he may have. He can be a jerk—as he was in that case—but I didn't call him a jerk. I called out his specific behavior and the effect it had on that little boy, and I told him so respectfully but candidly and firmly. He is a good man deep down. I think you saw the good side of him at the end. Eleanor Roosevelt once said, "To handle yourself, use your head. To handle others, use your heart." That's sort of what I did what with Big Dude.'"

Holbrook jotted down in his journal the phrase "treat issues coldly and people warmly." He seemed to study it for a moment before saying, "Thank you, Lano," still not realizing he had not gotten Lino's name right.

Lino left Stuart Holbrook's office realizing he had never spoken more than two words to the owner before, and yet he had just had a good thirty-minute conversation that was quite pleasant. He also realized that, as Todd said about Big Dude McGuire, there was something inside Mr. Holbrook's heart that was good but difficult for him to show and that perhaps very few people, if anyone, had ever seen.

"He is a good man deep down," Lino said to himself about the owner as he walked down the stairs to his travel office on the second floor. He was reminded of something he once read that said: "Be kind, for everyone you meet is fighting a hard battle." He got to his office and wrote Mr. Holbrook an e-mail thanking him for his time and passing along this last quote.

Stuart Holbrook immediately added that quote in his journal after reading Lino's e-mail, finally realizing his name was Lino, not Lano. But he didn't really care.

Joe Ferretti, Head Groundskeeper

Four hours before game time, Joe Ferretti had already spent six hours at the ballpark with his crew of fifteen people getting the field into game shape. Joe was proud of the work he and his crew did to maintain what many considered one of the best-landscaped baseball fields in the major leagues.

He could not remember a time when Stuart Holbrook actually stepped foot on the baseball field. Yet there was the owner, walking directly toward him.

"Oh no," mumbled Joe to himself, "what is this about?" Of course, Joe expected only the worst. He despised Stuart Holbrook, as did everyone else he knew who was associated with the ball club.

"Are you in charge?" asked Holbrook as he approached, again not knowing the name of the head groundskeeper of this meticulous ballpark.

"Yes, sir; I am Joe Ferretti, the head groundskeeper. How are you, Mr. Holbrook?" Joe could not remember the last time he had such a nervous stomach. It was the first time he had ever met the owner. His boss reported to the general manager, and he wondered why his boss or the GM were not here if there was a problem.

"Did you say your name was Jay?"

"Well, it's actually Joe, Mr. Holbrook."

"Oh, OK. Well, I need to talk to you for a few minutes," said Stuart without any regard as to whether the head ground-skeeper had any sense of urgency preparing the field with the game just a few hours away.

Joe noticed a journal of some sort and a pen in the owner's hand.

"Tell me what you know about Todd Ferragamo," said the owner, getting right to the point.

Without thinking of the consequences, Joe reacted immediately. "You're not thinking of trading him, are you, Mr. Holbrook?" He immediately realized he might have been out of line.

"No, I'm not thinking of trading him. I just want to know what your interactions have been with Ferragamo," Holbrook responded coldly. This employee had no business making such assumptions and questioning his motives.

"Well, what I can say is that every member of the ground crew loves the guy. He seems to pay as much attention to each one of us as he does his teammates. In fact, he knows the name of every one of my crew and knows about each person's life. He knows what college they've gone to, their personal interests and career ambitions, and basically everything that is important to each of them. They all talk about how encouraging he is about their goals and ambitions."

"Anything else?"

"Well, he's always complimenting me about the work we do and how, of all the major-league ballparks he plays in, our park is the best. That means a lot to me and the crew."

"Thank you. What's your name again?"

"J—"

Holbrook suddenly remembered. "Thank you, Joe."

As Holbrook closed his journal, Joe remembered something he'd read by Dale Carnegie, and he shared it with the owner. "'You can make more friends in two months by showing interest in others than you can in two years trying to get others interested in you.' That's what Todd does naturally."

Stuart reopened his journal, made note of that quote, and nodded as he walked away.

Kevin Scott, Manager of the Team

After meeting with Joe Ferretti, Stuart had his limo take him to the airport to fly to a board meeting with one of the Silicon Valley software companies in which he owned a 60 percent share. With limited time, he e-mailed the manager of his team, Kevin Scott: "Kevin, I'm curious about why Todd Ferragamo, a utility player all these years, has been elected captain of our team for the last few years. Thanks."

That evening, the team lost 5–3 to the Baltimore Orioles. It just so happened that Todd Ferragamo substituted for the starting third baseman. Twice he came to the plate with runners in scoring position; both times he failed to deliver. In the fourth inning, Todd was up with runners on second and third with two outs. He struck out swinging. In the seventh inning, he came to the plate with the bases loaded and one out. He grounded into a double play. Todd had the potential to drive in at least four runs in this game, and he failed.

When the game was over, Todd simply told the reporters, "I take full responsibility for the loss. I had the opportunity twice to do my job and bring in the necessary runs, and I failed. I apologize to my teammates and to the fans. I let everyone down. I let myself down."

The next morning, Kevin Scott went to the ballpark in preparation for a game later that day. He read and responded to Stuart Holbrook's e-mail:

Dear Mr. Holbrook,

Your question is an interesting one and is something I can talk about as I see Todd almost every day. Here is what I see in Ferragamo and why I believe the players elect him captain each year:

He steps up all the time to take the lead, whether it is to help our coaches during pregame practice, to advise me on the bench during the game, or to give candid but respectful feedback to a teammate or a needed pat on the back to a struggling player. His focus is on the team, each player, and the coaching staff. Besides being a major-league baseball player, he's a man of integrity. People trust him. He's a natural leader.

He takes responsibility for his failures and doesn't blame anyone. As a utility player he doesn't play all the time, so it's hard to keep his timing keen, but he will never use that as an excuse.

He gives credit to his teammates when they do something exceptional. In fact, I have seen him praise the ground crew, our traveling secretary, and the clubhouse attendants. If necessary, he will act as a coach to his teammates and provide tough feedback as well. He makes it his priority to see that each of his teammates thrives, and he strives to be the best he can be. He told me that managers in baseball are no different from managers in business—that a leader acts as a coach, not a boss. Managers in business can learn from Todd.

He is the only one with the courage to give direct and candid feedback when it's necessary, yet he does it in a way that is palatable. Yes, he even gives feedback to me and the coaches if necessary.

Todd treats everyone with dignity: his teammates, the coaches, and every employee for this organization, from the ground crew to the clubhouse attendant. And the fans are treated with appreciation, too.

Finally, I would say he looks at the greater good, what is best for the organization and the team, not just what is best for him personally. Most players in this league look at what is best for them at the expense of the team. Not Todd. And he has every reason to be selfish and think of himself as he doesn't play much.

Stuart Holbrook read the e-mail on his mobile phone and saved it. He was learning more and more about the leadership skills of Todd Ferragamo and how his leadership skills were really life skills, not the leadership skills in books or learned at seminars that talked about things like creating a vision or having followers, or something conceptual or theoretical. In fact, Stuart was realizing that Todd created more leaders because he modeled effective, trust-based, and character-based leadership.

As Stuart thought further, he was realizing that Todd's leadership skills were based on fundamentals of everyday life: character, integrity, taking responsibility for failures, giving credit to others for successes, stepping up when no one else bothered to, and finally, treating every person with dignity.

As Holbrook jotted these conclusions in his journal, something was happening to this billionaire executive. He was beginning to feel inspired for the first time in years.

Eric Cianciulli, Sports Reporter for the Largest City Newspaper

About two weeks after the long road trip ended and the team was back home, Stuart Holbrook got a call from Eric Cianciulli (Chan-chu-lee), a veteran sportswriter for the *Herald* who had been following the team for seventeen years. Eric had seen hundreds of players come and go. He was a walking encyclopedia of knowledge and insight about all the players, the coaches, and the last four managers of the team. Of course, Eric Cianciulli had opinions about Stuart Holbrook as well. He compared the owner to Ebenezer Scrooge, the infamous character from Charles Dickens's *A Christmas Carol.* It seemed Holbrook treated people no differently than Scrooge treated his devoted worker Bob Cratchit, the father of Tiny Tim.

Eric placed a call to Stuart Holbrook to get his views about an article he was writing about trade rumors of some of the players. Of course, Todd Ferragamo was not part of the trade rumors. What value could he bring to a team with his dismal career as a utility player? After denying any rumors, Stuart opened his top drawer and grabbed his journal; he wanted to use this opportunity to get the beloved sportswriter's perspective on Ferragamo.

"So, Eric, to change the subject, I have a question for you."

"Sure, Mr. Holbrook." No one was ever allowed to call Holbrook by his first name, even a veteran writer such as Eric Cianciulli.

"What do you think of Todd Ferragamo?"

"Well, he knows the game, is not bad defensively, and—"

"No, I mean as a person."

Eric didn't have to hesitate. "The first word that comes to my mind is 'Leader,' with a capital *L*."

Holbrook had his pen ready to write in his journal. "Why do you say that?"

"I've never seen a guy with such character, a quiet strength—kind but strong—a person who treats every person he sees the same. It is as simple as that. He's not the leader you read about who creates visions and markets himself, seeks publicity, and says one thing publicly and another behind the scenes. His leadership is what I would call character based. I'm willing to bet that Todd treats you the same way he treats the person who serves him coffee at Dunkin' Donuts."

Stuart was really starting to get it now. "TREAT PEOPLE WITH DIGNITY!" he wrote in large letters.

"And one final thing, Mr. Holbrook."

"Yes, Eric?"

"I once asked him how he made captain when he is a utility player, someone who shows up every game and sits on the bench."

"How did he respond?"

"He said, 'Eric, if you treat your job as important, it is likely to return the favor. I treat my role as a utility player as important. I guess it has returned the favor. Go figure, huh? I'm sure the same applies to you. I can see you take your job seriously, and it's paid you back with all your success as the top sports-media personality in the city.'

"He's the most humble person I have ever met. Combining his humility with the level of dignity he gives every person he interacts with is what makes him a great leader and why people love him and respect him. It is his character."

"This was very helpful to me, Eric. Thank you."

Eric was shocked he even got a thank-you, but he was even more shocked by what Stuart Holbrook said next. "And Eric, please call me Stuart."

Eric noticed a different tone in the man's voice.

Stuart Holbrook hung up the phone, read his notes again, and felt something changing inside him. And it made him happy.

Nick "Big Dude" McGuire, The Superstar

Ninety minutes before the start of the evening game against the Chicago White Sox, Stuart stunned everyone by doing something he had never done before. He was walking around talking to the players, showing personal interest, and treating each one respectfully. Nick "Big Dude" McGuire was paranoid as he stood getting ready to take his batting practice round. He was expecting the sour-faced owner to mention in his usual fiercely direct way the $23 million-per-year salary Nick was receiving and what the team was getting—or rather not getting—in return for the salary. As "Big Dude" was loosening up with practice swings with the weighted bat, he noticed Mr. Holbrook and some of his teammates gathered by the dugout actually smiling and laughing together.

"Oh no," he said aloud to himself, "now what? If he mentions my salary again, or if he puts me down, I'm gonna say something. I can't take his crap no matter how much they pay me." Holbrook had told Big Dude over and over how his yearly salary was the same as what Holbrook paid for the whole team years ago. And it was rumored that Big Dude used enhancement drugs to affect his home-run totals, so he was dealing not just with pressure from the inimitable Stuart Holbrook to justify his salary but also with stress from the league about the drug testing. Life wasn't happy for McGuire, no matter how much he was earning.

"Hello, son," said Stuart Holbrook in a tone totally unlike his usual one. "How's the Dude Man?" Holbrook was never in a mood like this.

Dude Man? Nick was definitely puzzled. "OK, Mr. Holbrook. I'm just getting ready for batting practice." Nick was looking at the owner, still puzzled and trying to read him to determine if he was being facetious or if this was a setup for another gratuitous remark.

"I see you've done pretty well these last few weeks, Nick. Very impressive. Are you back at the top of the home-run leaders now? I think you actually lead both leagues in home runs, correct?"

"I think so, sir." Nick knew he was leading but was attempting to be somewhat humble in front of the owner.

"Well, good for you, son. I'm proud of you. You're an asset to this team, and I want you to know how much I appreciate your efforts and production. You are a big part of the reason why we won nine of our last eleven games." Stuart actually felt good saying that. He quickly realized how good it feels to say something encouraging to someone.

"Thanks, Mr. Holbrook." Nick had never had this type of interaction with the owner. It was the first time he did not feel defensive, or intimidated, or nervous being around the boss.

"Nick, I have a question for you, if you could, please."

Nick had also never heard a "please" come from the owner.

"Do you think Todd Ferragamo is a good captain?"

"Absolutely, Mr. Holbrook," he said without hesitation. "You wanna know why?"

"Of course, Nick. I value your opinion, since you're one of the superstars in the league."

By now, Big Dude was at ease but still amazed at the personality transformation of the man who had such a notorious reputation in the league.

"Todd's leadership comes from his character, which is full of integrity and humility." Nick noticed that Mr. Holbrook took a journal out of his suit jacket and opened it up and started writing.

"Oh, you don't mind if I take notes, Nick, do you?" Stuart said.

Nick was more puzzled than ever. Here was the owner asking permission to take notes, actually listening, and seemingly valuing what he had to say.

"Of course not, sir."

"Nick, please call me Stuart."

Nick was still nowhere ready to call one of the world's wealthiest men and the owner of the team by his first name.

"So you mentioned his character, integrity, and humility? What do you mean by those?"

"Well, Mr. Holbrook, Todd has a natural way of being honest with me, and with all of us on the team. He's a straight shooter."

Stuart remembered what he'd heard from Lino Fernandez and asked, "You mean like treating issues coldly and people warmly?"

"Yes! Exactly! He can convey a tough message and do it in the most respectful way. It takes courage to be honest and give candid feedback to others, and Todd does it his own, natural way."

"OK, thanks, Nick. Go on, please."

"And when I say 'humility,' he is the first to take complete responsibility if he didn't do his job—like how many times if he made an error or didn't get the hit with a runner on base, or we lost a game, he would stand up and take responsibility for not contributing. He'd take the burden off the pitcher and put the responsibility on himself. People who meet him cannot believe he is a professional athlete.

"You should see the way he talks to the fans! He treats everybody as if they were the most important person in the world. And he encourages everyone he comes in contact with to be the best they can be. I once heard him encouraging a fan who was trying to figure out what to do with his life, and I remember Todd providing this person with a quote that I still remember to do this day. He quoted Saint Francis de Sales, who said, 'Be who you are and be it well.'"

"So you feel it's his character, treating each person with dignity, his humility by taking responsibility, and even taking the hit for his teammates when he himself could have done better?"

"Yes, sir. And when it is about him, he passes any credit directed his way and directs it toward others. He seems to love seeing others shine while he stays in the background. All of that, to me, Mr. Holbrook, is what makes Todd a great captain. He's more than a captain; he's a leader who's like an extra coach on the team. I remember he told me something, and I asked him to write it down because I would never remember it. I keep it in my locker. Hold on, I'll go get it."

Big Dude went to the clubhouse and looked inside his disorganized locker, found the quote, and ran back out to read it to Stuart. "Here it is, Mr. Holbrook. Todd told me it is from an ancient Chinese philosopher named Lao-Tse, from the sixth century BC, who said, 'A leader is best when people barely know he exists. When his work is done, his aim fulfilled, they will say, "We did this ourselves."'"

"Wow, thanks so much, Nick. This is helpful. By the way, I'm doing this because I know I've been a terrible leader. I'm in my role only because of my wealth. I know I've been hard on you, Nick, but I want you to know that I think you're a good man and an incredible talent. I'm grateful to have you on our team. You're Big Dude! Our Big Dude!"

For the first time ever, Nick felt he was much more than a superstar athlete, but someone who felt valued by the owner and the organization. He felt like he was part of a team. It was a turning point for Nick McGuire's professional career, and it had nothing to do with his statistics. It had to do with being a legitimate part of something bigger—the team and the organization.

It was also another step for Stuart Holbrook, who was realizing more and more how good it felt to encourage people, treat them with dignity, and make them feel valued.

Sean Patrick Kennedy, Security Guard

Two weeks later, the team returned from a short road trip to Cleveland and New York. It was a Monday-night game, and Sean Patrick Kennedy, the security guard in charge of the players' parking area on the side of the ballpark, was at work, allowing Todd Ferragamo and his modest four-year-old Ford Explorer into the parking area. Right behind him was Stuart Holbrook's limousine.

Todd parked his car, got out, and gave a friendly wave to the owner. "Hello, Stuart! Are you coming to the ballpark to have hot dogs for dinner again? The hot dogs are good here! Expensive but good!"

Todd was expecting the typical expressionless look on Stuart Holbrook's face. He was surprised when he heard the owner retort, "How did you know? I might even have two tonight. I get them for free!" With that, Sean and Todd heard Stuart laugh for the first time in their lives.

Todd was approaching Sean Patrick, whom he always affectionately called "SP." "Hey, SP, how is the 'fightin' Irishman' tonight?" Todd was referring not only to Sean Patrick's Irish ancestry but to his earlier days as an amateur boxer and to his lifelong obsession with his favorite college football team, the Notre Dame Fighting Irish.

Stuart Holbrook decided to observe a typical Todd Ferragamo interaction with yet another member of the organization, Sean Patrick Kennedy, a loyal and reliable ten-year employee.

"How are you today, sir?" said Sean to Todd Ferragamo.

"Come on, SP, how many times have we talked about not calling me 'sir'? If you call me 'sir,' I will call you 'sir.' God knows, you deserve that title a lot more than me."

"No, sir. You're a professional athlete and captain of this team. You deserve it."

"SP, I play a game, a child's game, and get paid far too much for providing little contribution to the world. You have a job with a lot more responsibility than any of us, providing security to the ballpark. The forty thousand fans in the park and the players with all these luxury cars depend on you, and so do I with my precious four-year-old Explorer that needs an oil change and tune-up badly."

Holbrook continued to watch and listen. "He gives every-one the time of day," Stuart was saying to himself, "and he does treat people with dignity."

"Listen, SP, has Rodge decided where he's going to college? Last time we talked, you mentioned it was either the University of New Hampshire or the University of Vermont."

Sean Patrick was amazed at how Todd took care to remem-ber the things that were important to him—in this case his son, Rodge. "He hasn't quite decided, and I'm getting ner-vous. He needs to decide as the application deadline is soon. I think it will come down to whichever school gives us the most financial aid."

"SP, here is my cell phone number. Have Rodge call me. I've visited both campuses and am happy to discuss this deci-sion with him, if that's OK."

"He would love to talk to you, Todd. But you're too busy."

"Are you kidding? Too busy? Doing what? Playing base-ball? I mean sitting on the bench every game?" responded Todd with self-effacing laughter. "Actually, better yet, give me Rodge's cell phone number, and I'll call him."

That Saturday, Todd and Rodge had a twenty-minute conversation about his college choice, his career ambitions, his father, and his girlfriends. Not one second was spent on Todd Ferragamo and his life as a professional baseball player.

Stuart Holbrook went to his office and recorded more notes in his journal, adding what he had just observed. And the following week, as he emerged from his car for another evening game, Stuart went up to the security guard and said, "Hello, Sean Patrick. Is it OK if I call you 'SP' as well?"

"Yes, of course, sir."

"Well, I want to thank you, SP, for all you do for this organization and the security you provide the players and the fans."

Sean Patrick Kennedy was another on a new list of amazed people who were seeing a different and more decent side of Stuart Holbrook for the first time.

"By the way, SP, did Todd ever talk to your son?"

"Yes, he did, Mr. Holbrook. He called him that weekend, and my son, Rodge hasn't stopped talking about it. The team captain had my son add his name as a reference for admission to both universities," said SP proudly.

"Yes, SP, he is a good team captain."

"May I be bold enough, sir, to add that he is the greatest leader I have ever seen," added Sean Patrick.

Stuart wanted to hear more to further his journey to becoming a better leader and a better man. "Why do you think that is?"

"Because," replied SP Kennedy with emotion visible in his face and voice, "he personifies the notion that people don't care how much you know until they know how much you care. He lifts people up every day with a simple hello and a look in the eye. I believe that sincerity is the face of the soul, and there is no better example of a sincere heart, a man of character, than Todd Ferragamo. He may not be an all-star, but he is everyone's all-star. I love my son, Rodge, and hope he turns out to be the man of character that Todd Ferragamo is."

"Thank you, SP. It's easy to see the love and pride you have for your son. He's a lucky young man to have a father like you as a role model."

SP Kennedy realized the goodness and the transformation of Stuart Holbrook, the man who was the Ebenezer Scrooge of bosses; he now seemed to be a man whose heart was filled with genuine goodness.

Stuart took the elevator to his office to write in his journal. He also made plans to provide a full scholarship to Rodge Kennedy to whatever college he chose.

Kiera Leahy, Veteran Flight Attendant on the Team's Charter; and Reginald Robinson

F ive days later the team boarded its Delta Airlines charter flight to the West Coast, the beginning of a ten-day road trip with eight games. Kiera Leahy was a thirty-one-year veteran flight attendant and one of the few selected by the airlines to fly the team charter flights. She loved this part of her job as it was so much different than the regular commercial flights. Now in her fifth year flying the team's charters, Kiera had gotten to know the players and coaches. She had seen many players come and go. She had never met Stuart Holbrook as he didn't associate with his players, plus he had his own private jet and crew. On this trip, however, Kiera saw a new face taking a seat in first class. She wasn't sure who it was until it was later confirmed by another flight attendant that it was indeed the team's owner. From everything she had heard about Holbrook over the years, she felt like she'd better be on her toes and try not to upset him; she heard he could be easily irritated and rude. But Kiera was a veteran, and she'd do her best to smile and not show any effects of ill behavior from someone who considered himself "mightier than thou."

"Hello, Kiera Diera!" Kiera was walking down the economy section of the plane when she heard the familiar voice of Todd Ferragamo. "How is the city's Irish Rose?"

"Todd, how are you? You still aren't taking your first-class seat? You're the team captain! When are you ever going to sit in first class?" said Kiera, knowing what the answer was going to be.

"I belong here with the team, Kiera," smiled Todd. He loved calling her "Kiera Diera," and she'd stopped being embarrassed by it a long time ago. "Besides, I gave my first-class seat to the father of one of our travel staff. He loves our team and has been a lifelong fan, and this is the first time he has ever flown in a plane, so it's going to be first class all the way." Todd was referring to Madison Robinson's father, Reginald, still in remission from cancer but now living a dream he never imagined—flying with his hometown professional baseball team in the team's charter and sitting in first class. "He's such a good man, a devoted husband and father. He deserves it. I hope I can be like him someday."

Kiera smiled and reminded herself again that she'd never met a more selfless man. "No wonder he's the captain and so well respected," she said to herself.

"How'd you get approval to have a fan travel with the team?" asked Kiera.

"I know the owner," smiled Todd with a wink.

"You mean Stuart Holbrook approved?" she was surprised. "From what I have always heard—" Todd put up his hand to stop her in midsentence.

"I know what you were going to say. In years past, I would have agreed with you, but Mr. Holbrook is a changed man. He has a good heart that no one knows about. Just watch. He has a great future ahead of him," said Todd knowing that a great future probably only meant another one to ten years, as the owner was seventy-seven years old. "Kiera, can you do me a favor, please?" asked Todd. This caught Kiera's attention because if there was one thing about Todd Ferragamo, it was that he was the least demanding passenger she'd ever experienced on her charter and commercial flights in thirty-one years.

Todd never wanted her to serve him, though that was her job. If he did anything to take her time on any of the flights, it was taking the time to talk to her about her career and experiences as a flight attendant, or about the husband she loved and her two daughters and son she adored, Brianna, Angela, and Zeike.

"Sure, Todd, anything for the team captain!" she responded.

"Take good care of Mr. Robinson. Let's create a great memory for him!" Kiera saw how excited it made Todd to know that someone so deserving was on the verge of a life memory—traveling with the team, staying in five-star hotels, sitting in box seats at the ballparks in Los Angeles and Seattle, and more. "And make sure Mr. Holbrook doesn't talk his ear off!" laughed Todd.

"You mean he is sitting next to—?"

"Yes, Stuart Holbrook." Todd smiled and winked again.

Kiera finished her tasks at the back end of the plane before taking her assignment in the first-class cabin, where she introduced herself to Stuart Holbrook and his guest, Reginald.

She noticed that Stuart Holbrook had a journal on his lap when he caught her attention. "Excuse me, Ms. Leahy?"

"Yes, sir."

"Oh, call me Stuart, please."

"Yes, Stuart?"

"I have a question. I'm curious about which player, in all your years traveling with the team, has had the greatest impact on you."

"That's an easy question, Stuart. It's Todd Ferragamo."

Stuart smiled. "Do you have a few minutes to explain why?"

Fifteen minutes later, as the last of the coaches finally were seated, Stuart had four more pages filled in his journal that explained why Todd Ferragamo, the team captain, was the greatest leader he ever saw.

Again, it all came down to the same attributes of good character: maintaining a person's dignity, showing selflessness and humility, treating issues coldly and people warmly, making an effort to listen and learn about others, being nice to each person because everyone is fighting a battle, and embodying the old Dale Carnegie lesson that "you can make more friends in two months by showing interest in others than you can in two years by trying to get others interested in you." Stuart was reminded that Todd treated everyone equally, like they taught in church, and that "a person who looks up to God rarely looks down on people."

Reginald Robinson was in such indescribable glory that he had to text his wife and daughter about this amazing adventure and how proud he was that his daughter, Madison, worked for such an incredible organization. He'd never had the opportunity to experience anything like this during his years of work and sweat and lack of appreciation.

Present Day

(moments after the World Series championship game)

Todd Ferragamo, Addie Ferragamo, and Stuart Holbrook

T odd was trying to run off the field, into the dugout, and into the locker room. He was stopped by the Fox Sports reporter with a microphone and waited until five of his teammates and the crew of Fox Sports basically pushed Todd to say a few words to the reporter.

"Todd Ferragamo!" said Christina Gonzaga, a young rising star with Fox Sports and the reporter with a global audience watching. "What a moment! You made history today! What was going through your mind as you rounded the bases with a walk-off home run to win the World Series?"

Todd thought for a second and said, "All I could think about was my dear sister, Adrielle—I called her Addie—who was the most decent person I ever met. She died young, and I will love and miss her for the rest of my life. I hope she was watching. She changed my life in a really profound way, and I am forever grateful."

Christina was at a loss to follow up with another question. Todd noticed she was touched, so he helped her out by adding, "I just got lucky today. I had no business hitting that ball out of the ballpark. Luis Martinez was overpowering me, so I knew the last pitch would be a fastball and that I'd have to start my swing a lot earlier to make contact. I was simply lucky. Though this was a big hit, each of my teammates played their hearts out all year, including in these last seven games. I'm proud of each of them, the coaches, and our incredible owner, Stuart Holbrook. This is a team win. I got the luckiest hit of my life, yet my teammates worked much harder than I did all year and in this series. I am proud of each and every one of them—"

"But describe the feeling of hitting this historic home run," Christina insisted.

"—and the coaching staff, starting with Kevin Scott," continued Todd to the Fox Sports reporter. "I've never seen another person who knows how to get the most out of his people.

"Businesses can learn from Kevin Scott. He got each person and the team as a whole to be all that we can be. It's no wonder the media refers to Kevin as a 'players' manager.' But forget about that. He epitomizes what leadership is all about by getting the most out of people and achieving results consistently and with integrity. I have to run, Christina. Thank you! And congratulations on a great career!" With that Todd finally managed to escape into the locker room.

A few minutes later, Todd sat in the corner of the locker room enjoying watching his teammates celebrate. He sat quietly with reporter Eric Cianciulli and talked off the record about the year they'd had and winning the World Series.

"When I travel in the off-season to places like Dubai and Europe, I realize the amusement the rest of the world has with Americans referring to our fall classic as the 'World Series,' since it is just an American series."

They both laughed. "That's true!" said Eric.

"So how do you enjoy your work and the newspaper, Eric?"

Eric was surprised to all of a sudden be the one answering questions instead of asking them. He thought a second and responded, "I enjoy the work, Todd, but working for this company is difficult. I'm not valued in many ways, even though I'm a veteran reporter. I get many offers to move to a different organization, a different paper, and maybe I should move. It amazes me, Todd, that after all these years with the same company, I don't feel valued."

"Well, you know, Eric, a man by the name of Robert McNamara once said, 'Brains are like hearts. They go where they are appreciated.' That says it all to me."

The cameras and reporters from Fox Sports, ESPN, and other stations around the world wanted Todd Ferragamo to step up for an interview, but he didn't want to focus the attention on himself as "the hero." He wanted the focus on his team for a hard-fought season of 162 games plus another 19 games in the playoffs and World Series championship. Todd knew he was the one the media wanted to talk to and not his fellow teammates. Some had battled through painful injuries the media never knew about, and others had battled personal issues outside of work to focus on performing in a high-stakes and stressful environment, where every mistake was headlined in the media. Todd had great admiration for those team members who demonstrated unwavering support and encouragement to other players. To Todd, they were all heroes. He had played in only 35 of the 162 games during the season and in only one game in the World Series.

"They deserve this celebration," Todd said to Eric. "You'll never know how hard they worked to get here and finally win."

With the pressure mounting for Todd to step up to the podium before the camera, he quickly went upstairs to relax and unwind in the general manager's office on the second floor. He took his clothes from his locker room and took a shower in the general manager's private bathroom. He wanted the limelight to fall where it was deserved, on his teammates who played day in and day out all season. He told his agent to decline all the early-morning television interviews so his other teammates could have the opportunity to shine on national TV.

Stuart Holbrook enjoyed watching the players pour champagne all over each other as they laughed and cried and let loose for the celebration. He knew it was a moment they'd never forget. He saw Todd Ferragamo sitting quietly talking to Eric Cianciulli, the reporter. Then he saw Todd disappear.

The players had come to love the man Stuart Holbrook had become over the last few years. The newer players were surprised to hear about the old Stuart because all they saw was a man who was selfless and seemed to know about each player: where he grew up, whether or not he had kids, and in many cases even the names of his wife and children. The media came to respect and admire the leader he had become, far more than they admired his wealth and business savvy.

Stuart had a feeling where Todd went.

Todd heard the knock on the door.

"Our captain! What a night, son. Congratulations! You shocked the world tonight! I want to just say one thing, Todd," said Stuart Holbrook as he entered the office and gave Todd a big fatherly hug.

"Yes, Stuart?"

"I am so proud of you. Not because of the home run, though, of course, this moment will go down in baseball history. I am proud of the man you are, the leader you are to every player on this team. In fact, you have turned my life around because you taught me the purpose of maintaining the dignity of every person." Stuart had tears in his eyes and was caught up more in the emotion of his life lessons over the last four years than he was in this incredible sports moment. "You taught me to be a better man. It took me too long to learn, but I am glad I finally did learn."

Todd saw how genuine the words were coming from a man who used to be universally recognized as the most arrogant man ever. Todd did not know what to say as he was too emotional thinking of the momentous event that had just occurred, his sister Addie, and now a profound compliment he was not expecting and felt he did not deserve because of the numerous flaws in himself he had to work on his whole life. "Thank you, Stuart," was all he could muster. "I'm glad we've gotten to be friends." Todd thought of something he had learned years ago that he felt applied to the man Holbrook had become. It said, "What you are is God's gift to you. What you make of yourself is your gift to God." Todd felt that Holbrook gave God a great gift with all his charitable organizations and the effect they were having on millions of people around the world. Todd was proud of how Holbrook's impact far outweighed his enormous wealth.

"Todd, as I was learning about leaders and observing what makes you such a great one, I came across something that Albert Schweitzer once said. He said, 'Every person I know who has been truly happy has learned how to serve others.' I am a truly happy man today," Holbrook said. "I was lost for so many years of my life. These last four years have given me a profound purpose in life, and the feeling is far more satisfying than even this World Series win."

Todd had nothing to say. He felt he was being given too much credit for the flawed man he felt he always was. All he could say was, "Thank you for insisting I stay on this team over the years. It was a very fair case that I not be on the team with my limited contribution and talent, so thank you."

"Todd," replied Stuart, "you contributed in ways the scorebook can never record. You were the captain, the leader, we needed. The bonus—and this is selfish of me—is that I learned about the significance and value of humility, character, and treating all people with dignity."

They watched the locker room celebration on the TV in the general manager's office while Todd quietly thanked God for his blessings in life, starting with the gift of experiencing a sister's love for her brother. It was Addie who always believed in him even when he was at his worst, who saw the goodness in his heart, who always forgave him, and who gave him unconditional love while being direct and candid with him. By modeling what integrity, humility, and goodness are all about, she did for Todd what Todd did for Stuart Holbrook and many others who came across his path in life: she taught him to be a leader. She taught him to be a better person, a person of character and decency. Todd still had many flaws, and deep down he knew all the good things he heard about himself were not completely accurate as he still caught himself dealing with moments of anger, making inappropriate remarks, and making wrong assumptions about the motives of others and therefore drawing wrong conclusions. He was as imperfect as any person. He simply tried to be a better man every single day.

When Eric Cianciulli met him sneaking out of the ballpark at two thirty in the morning, he asked Todd if he could give him something to write about in the newspaper the next day. Todd had already thought about it. "Sure, Eric, what would you like to ask?"

"What went through your mind as you rounded the bases with one of the most historic home runs in baseball history?"

"I thought of my sister, Addie, who died too young. She had an amazing ability to forgive and an amazing ability to lift me up and love me as unconditionally as a sister could love a brother. I was thinking what an amazing life I have while hers was cut short before she ever married or had children or a career. So, Eric, I dedicate this moment in my life to my sister, Addie. It's for her because otherwise I wouldn't be a professional athlete. More importantly, she turned my life around from drugs, alcohol, arrogance and hubris, and bullying and taught me life lessons that I still try to live every day."

"Thank you for sharing that, Todd. Can I can write that?"

"Of course you can. I want the world to know the amazing person my sister was. This is her time to get in the spotlight."

"Anything else?"

"Well, I'm just a very lucky guy who's playing a game for a living. I did one big thing in my career—this home run—and yet I have teammates who play every day with physical pain you'll never know about and deal with tough personal issues, and they give their heart and soul to this team and this city. They deserve far more recognition than me. I am considered a hero for having that moment that every player wishes they had. But these guys, my teammates I am referring to, are the unsung heroes who never get mentioned. They worked so hard for this to happen. They got us here, not me. I just got lucky with one swing where I barely saw the ball. My leg was shaking like crazy. Make sure you recognize the heart and sweat these guys put in all year. I'm proud to be part of this team, Eric."

Three months later, after seventeen years with the same newspaper, Eric Cianciulli landed a prime reporting role with a 40 percent pay increase and stock options with the across-town competitor. When people asked him why he left after such a long tenure with the same organization, he replied, "Brains are like hearts. They go where they are appreciated."

Epilogue

Stuart Holbrook

Stuart Holbrook, the shrewd and formerly self-absorbed billionaire businessman, had left his mark over the last twelve years of his life. He would donate 95 percent of his wealth, which he realized was a blessing from God, for the betterment of humanity, leaving billions of dollars anonymously to cancer research, Lou Gehrig's disease research, diabetes research, and two hospital wings in Chicago and Boston.

He set up an overarching global foundation called the Foundation for Human Dignity, which consisted of more than fifteen foundations, all with the mission to "promote human dignity in the world" but in different ways. His anonymous donations totaled $5 billion, and his foundations were capitalized at over $17 billion. The foundations consisted of scholarships for grade schools, high schools, and colleges for inner-city children from low-income families. New schools were built, none using Stuart Holbrook's name. Adult education centers, recreation centers, and many more community assets were built, none using his name. Some scholarships were based on scholastic achievement, while others were awarded to elementary and high school students for demonstrations of selflessness and random acts of kindness. There was even a foundation that eventually built seventy-two hundred new homes for the poorest of the poor across the United States and in countries like Sudan, Nigeria, Haiti, the Dominican Republic, the Philippines, Thailand, and India. There was another fund for global victims of major natural disasters such as earthquakes, tsunamis, and extreme weather.

When he died at age eighty-five, Stuart Holbrook was remembered as a man who changed the world, who transformed himself into one of the greatest leaders the world had seen. He achieved results with integrity and treated every person he met—rich or poor, powerful or humble—with dignity, consistently demonstrating a servant's heart. He had realized that his wealth, accomplishments, and, most important, the foundation so close to his heart, were not achieved by himself alone.

He practiced another lesson Todd Ferragamo once taught him: "always keep developing know-how and know-who." With his "know-who," he leveraged his network of relationships to build the idea of the foundation into a reality. He read about the life of Jesus and the life of the Prophet Mohammed. Basically, he learned more about God and his love. In the Koran, he learned about God's view of charity and goodwill, such as the verse from Surah 2–Al Baqarah, which says, "Whatever you spend of good must be for parents and kindred and orphans and the needy and the wayfarer. And whatever you do of good deeds—truly Allah (God) knows it well." From the Bible, especially Proverbs 4:23, he learned to live his life: "Guide your heart above all else, for it determines the course of your life."

In his will, Stuart named Todd Ferragamo as the executive director of the Human Dignity Foundation. Stuart justified his choice by saying, "This foundation deserves a strong leader—a person who will achieve results with integrity, who has a servant's heart, and who models how to treat all people with dignity. That man is Todd Ferragamo because in all my years in boardrooms with the wealthiest and most powerful, from Hollywood to Washington, from Wall Street to the sports world, Mr. Ferragamo was the greatest leader I ever saw."

When he learned of this appointment, Todd had been retired for six years, living a quiet and unassuming life and doing what he had always done—building people up. Todd had not yet married, but he hoped he would someday find a wonderful woman to love and show devotion to, and hopefully he'd have a son or a daughter to love and to teach lessons like his sister Addie had taught him. In the meantime, he continued to surround himself with a wide circle of friends.

Todd was moved by Holbrook's appointment and honored to take on the executive director's position.

One of Todd Ferragamo's first decisions was to rename the foundation the Stuart Holbrook Foundation for Human Dignity.

He continued to dedicate his work and the mission of the foundation to the person he loved the most and who influenced his life most powerfully: his sister, Addie.

Twenty-Five Character-Based Leadership Lessons From the Greatest Leader He Ever Saw

(in order as they appear in the story)

1. "Leadership is about achieving results consistently and doing so with integrity" (Michael F. Andrew, *How to Think like a CEO and Act like a Leader*).
2. "Be more concerned with your character than your reputation because your character is what you really are, while your reputation is merely what others think you are" (Coach John Wooden, UCLA).
3. "Courage is not the absence of fear. It is taking action in the presence of fear" (John F. Kennedy, *Profiles in Courage*).
4. "Don't ever mistake one's kindness for weakness" (unknown).
5. "How you treat people from all walks of life ultimately says everything about you" (Michael F. Andrew).
6. "My religion is simple. My religion is kindness" (Dalai Lama).
7. "People who look up to God rarely look down on people" (unknown).

8. People don't care how much you know until they know how much you care" (President Theodore Roosevelt).

9. "Treat issues coldly and people warmly" (Michael F. Andrew, *How to Think like a CEO and Act like a Leader*).

10. "To handle yourself, use your head. To handle others, use your heart" (Eleanor Roosevelt, former first lady of the United States).

11. "Be kind, for everyone you meet is fighting a hard battle" (Plato).

12. "You can make more friends in two months by showing sincere interest in others than you can in two years trying to get people interested in you" (Dale Carnegie).

13. "A leader acts as a coach, not as a boss" (Michael F. Andrew).

14. "Put the greater good first, such as your family, the organization, your staff, or your team" (Michael F. Andrew).

15. "If you treat your job as important, it is likely to return the favor" (unknown).

16. "Be who you are and be it well" (Saint Francis de Sales).

17. "A leader is best when people barely know he exists. When his work is done, his aim fulfilled, they will say, 'We did this ourselves'" (Lao Tse).

18. "Brains are like hearts. They go where they are appreciated" (Robert McNamara, former CEO of Ford Motor Company and former secretary of defense).

19. "What you are is God's gift to you. What you make of yourself is your gift to God" (Unknown).

20. "Every person I know who has been truly happy has learned how to serve others" (Albert Schweitzer).

21. "Keep enhancing your know-how and your know-who" (Michael F. Andrew, *How to Think like a CEO and Act like a Leader*).

22. "Whatever you spend of good must be for parents and kindred and orphans and the needy and the wayfarer. And whatever you do of good deeds—truly Allah (God) knows it well" (Koran, Surat 2–Al Baqarah).

23. "Guide your heart above all else, for it determines the course of your life" (Old Testament, Prov. 4:23).

Other Lessons

24. Integrity, humility, and treating people with dignity are the foundations of great character-based leaders (Michael F. Andrew).

25. There is a difference between leadership and boss-ship. Leaders serve others. Bosses are self-serving (Michael F. Andrew, *How to Think like a CEO and Act like a Leader*).

Questions

1. What leadership lesson(s) in the book resonated with you the most? Why?

2. Which leadership lesson will you start applying immediately? How will you do so?

3. Who is the best leader or manager you ever worked for? Why was he or she the best and what did you learn from him or her as a leader or manager?

4. Why do you think character and integrity are fundamental to leadership?

5. How do *you* define "leadership"?

About the Author

A global executive and a leadership thought leader with degrees from three US universities, Michael F. Andrew is the author of the book *How to Think like a CEO and Act like a Leader*, which has generated impressive reviews on Amazon and was featured on *Fox Morning News* in Boston. He is currently the chief talent and leadership development officer and an executive committee member for one of the most respected private companies in Saudi Arabia.

Michael was the group vice president for a multibillion-dollar global telecom headquartered in the United Arab Emirates, where he also served as a board advisory member for the company's academy. As a business owner and consultant, Mike led efforts with multinational firms in creating and implementing executive development initiatives built around each company's strategic imperatives and pressing business challenges. He has coached corporate executives and McKinsey consultants around the world and has authored articles in leading magazines such as *Chief Learning Officer, CEO Middle East,* and *Talent Magazine.*

You can view Michael's appearance on *Fox Morning News* at http://www.leadershipauthor.com.

https://www.linkedin.com/in/mikeandrew11